JB
CABEZA DE VACA

DATE

Cabeza de Vaca

Conquistador Who Cared

by

MARY DODSON WADE

COLOPHON HOUSE HOUSTON, TEXAS

*For Betty, who has made
her own journey across the Southwest with us*

NOTE: Places with names appearing in THIS TYPE FACE in the text were established after the time of Cabeza de Vaca or were not known by that name at the time.

Cataloging-in-Publication Data

Wade, Mary Dodson
Cabeza de Vaca; Conquistador Who Cared/by Mary Dodson Wade
96p. maps bibliog.

Summary: A biography of the Spanish conquistador who survived a failed mission to Florida to spend seven years among Indians in the American Southwest. He then tried to secure humane treatment of the Indians during a disastrous term as governor of the lower half of the South American continent.
1.Núñez Cabeza de Vaca, Álvar, ca 1490-1556 2.America-Discovery and Exploration-Spanish 3.Paraguay-History-to 1811 4.Explorers-America-Biography 5.Indians of North America [1.Núñez Cabeza de Vaca, Álvar 2.Indians of North America 3.America-Discovery and Exploration 4.South America-History] I. Title
ISBN 1-882539-14-1
ISBN 1-882539-15-X (pbk)
F125.N9 W33 1995
910.92
[B]

"Regarding the Journey
I Made . . ."

Nearly 500 years ago five ships left a harbor near Cadiz, Spain, to seek fame and wealth in the New World. Its mission was to claim all the land around the GULF OF MEXICO for the king of Spain.

Just a few years earlier Hernán Cortés had subdued the Aztecs in New Spain (MEXICO), and Francisco Pizarro was shortly to do the same to the Incas in Peru. Pánfilo de Narváez had dreams that Florida would bring him success and riches, but that did not happen. While Spanish ships crisscrossed the Atlantic Ocean carrying gold and silver to his majesty King Charles V, this expedition not only failed to find gold, it was not even able to establish a colony.

Eight years after the Narváez expedition left Spain, four survivors walked into Mexico City with the incredible story of what had happened to them. Álvar Núñez Cabeza de Vaca, second in command on the expedition, returned to Spain. On the fiftieth anniversary of Christopher Columbus's first voyage to the Western Hemisphere, he published the story of those who survived the ordeal.

Tales of the New World fascinated the Spaniards. One story which fired their imaginations concerned five priests who had supposedly sailed westward centuries before. The legend persisted that they had found a place called Antigua where there were seven cities filled with hordes of gold. Cabeza de Vaca's report recounted the hardships he endured as he walked across the lower part of the North American continent. There was no mention of the Seven Cities of Gold, but that did not squelch the Spaniards's obsession with finding fabulous gold treasure.

Cabeza de Vaca apologized to the king for his lack of success, but the real value of his report was the information he gave Europeans about the New World. He described the terror and destruction of hurricanes — storms that were unknown to them. He pictured for them animals they had never seen — opossums and American bison. He detailed the food, houses, and habits of Indian tribes that lived in the territory through which he had walked.

He brought no gold to the king, but in the end he provided much more. He proved that the interior of North America was land, not water. He opened a continent no one knew was there.

Amazingly, Cabeza de Vaca returned to the New World several years later as governor of the lower half of South America. This adventure, no less disastrous than the first, brought him home in chains.

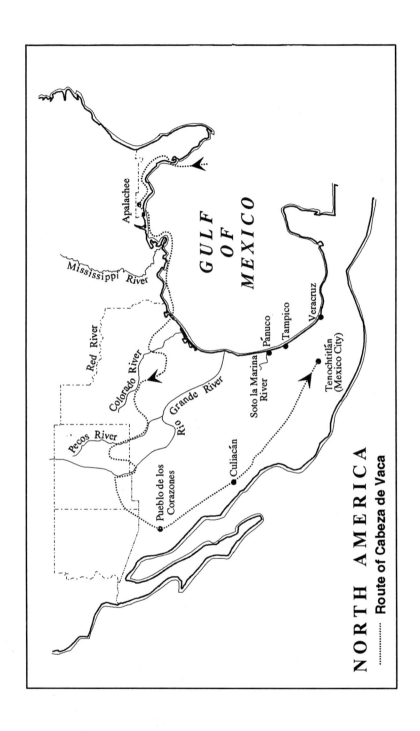

NORTH AMERICA
.... Route of Cabeza de Vaca

"Five Ships in which Went
Six Hundred Men"

In *June 1527 five ships* stood in the harbor of
Sanlúcar de Barrameda on the southwest tip of Spain.
The Narváez expedition was ready to sail. Pánfilo de
Narváez, a fiery, one-eyed redhead, had outfitted the
ships with his own money. He held the title of Governor
of Florida, an area that extended from the tip of the
Florida peninsula westward to New Spain.

Second in command of the expedition was a
thirty-seven-year-old conquistador named Álvar Núñez

Cabeza de Vaca, a native of Jerez de la Frontera in the southern province of Cadiz.

Cabeza de Vaca, the oldest of four children, had been born about 1490 to parents from prominent families. On his father's side, his grandfather, Pedro de Vera, had led a cruel conquest of the Canary Islands. However, he deliberately chose not to use the surname of his father, Francisco de Vera, but chose instead that of his mother, Doña Teresa Cabeza de Vaca.

The source of the unusual name, Cabeza de Vaca, had come three hundred years earlier. One of his mother's ancestors, a peasant named Martin Alhaja, had helped the king of Navarre defeat Muslim forces at the Battle of Las Navas de Tolosa in 1212. The shepherd had placed cow skulls to mark an unguarded pass through the Sierra Morena mountains, making it possible for the Spaniards to surprise the Moors in an ambush. In appreciation the king bestowed on the family the name meaning "the head of a cow."

Orphaned early, Cabeza de Vaca was sent to live with an uncle on his father's side. Because the family held positions of prominence, the boy had advantages that came with social position. He learned to read and write but was no scholar.

While still a teenager, he joined the army. In 1511 he accompanied King Ferdinand's army when it went to the aid of Pope Julius II in Italy. The following year he survived the Battle of Ravenna where 20,000 soldiers were killed. He was back in Spain ten years later in the service of the Duke of Medina Sidonia and distinguished himself during a number of major battles.

He participated in the capture of the Alcázar, the three-hundred-fifty-year-old Moorish seat of government in Seville, in a battle which led to the ouster of the Moors from the area. For this, he was honored with responsibility of guarding one of the city gates and entrusted with messages for the king, who was in Valladolid in the northern interior of the country.

Now, in 1527, Charles V, King of Spain and Emperor of the Holy Roman Empire, showed his confidence in the career soldier by giving him royal appointment as second in command of the mission to settle Florida. His duties were that of treasurer and also *alguacil mayor*, the person in charge of seeing that justice was done in military disputes. His even temper later in the face of extreme hardships proved the king had made a good choice, but having relatives in the government probably played a bigger role in his appointment.

Displaying a characteristic lack of prejudice, he married Maria de Marmolejo shortly before leaving on the voyage to Florida. Her aristocratic family in Seville was connected to both Christians and Jews.

In contrast, the commander of the expedition, Pánfilo de Narváez, was often the center of controversy. He was twenty years older than Cabeza de Vaca and had already been to the New World, where his actions

9

against the Indians in Cuba gained him a reputation for extreme cruelty.

From Cuba, Narváez went to New Spain to arrest Hernán Cortés, who had invaded MEXICO in violation of the orders of his commander. He lost the sight of one eye in the clash between their two forces. Then, as if his wounds were not enough, he watched his defeated forces readily join the opposing side. Narváez returned to Spain determined to receive a command where he could find riches equal to those of the conqueror of the Aztecs.

That prize seemed in sight. He now held a commission from Charles V entitling him to settle an area bordering the GULF OF MEXICO. Sixteenth-century maps marked this body of water as the Sea of the North. The maps correctly showed New Spain's land mass as curving to the east and gave the body of water north of it the name Sea of the North. The GULF OF CALIFORNIA, actually on the west, was placed south of it and therefore earned the name Sea of the South.

As governor of Florida, Narváez had the task of bringing under Spain's rule all the inhabitants living along the upper shore of the Sea of the North. The area stretched westward from the Florida Cape to the Río de las Palmas. This river has now known as the SOTO LA MARINA. It is north of Tampico, in the Mexican state of TAMAULIPAS. Tampico, founded by Cortés, was near the northern limit of New Spain, and the area near the river was referred to as Pánuco.

As obstinate as he was short-sighted, Narváez exercised little caution in his performance as commander. In the end, his ill-advised actions cost him his life and doomed the expedition to failure.

Three other officers sailed with the expedition. Alonso Enríquez was purser, with responsibility for keeping a record of accounts. Acting as quartermaster and tax agent for the king was Alonso de Solís. The *commissario* was Fray Juan Suárez of the Order of St. Francis. Father Suárez, whose title put him in charge of religious affairs in foreign provinces, was one of five Franciscan priests on board.

A large number of the passengers were foot soldiers, along with some cavalrymen. Captain Alonso del Castillo Maldonado commanded one group of soldiers. Castillo, the son of a doctor and a noblewoman from the city of Salamanca, would survive the expedition.

Andrés Dorantes de Carranza was another man whose luck held. A resident of the city of Gibraleón, Dorantes was accompanied by his cousins, Diego Dorantes and Pedro de Valdivieso. The cousins did not survive.

All levels of society sailed with the expedition, including servants of the wealthy. Dorantes had his slave Estevánico. The dark Arab, whose color was described as brown by one who had seen him, was a native of Azamor, MOROCCO, on the west coast of North Africa near CASABLANCA. Estevánico would live through the eight-year ordeal, only to be sent back as a scout for Francisco Vásquez de Coronado when that conquistador went looking for the Seven Cities of Cibola.

Interestingly enough, a native of the New World was aboard. A prince with the Spanish name Don Pedro was travelling with Father Suárez. Perhaps he had gone to Spain with Father Suárez, who had taken part in Cortés's conquest of Mexico. The prince may have been Pedro Tetlahuehuezquiziti, brother of King Ixtlilxochitl, who had helped Cortés defeat the Aztecs. Whatever his Indian name, Don Pedro never reached home.

Rounding out the "more or less" six hundred passengers were ten women who accompanied their husbands. These families came to be part of the permanent settlement Narváez was to establish. Before their departure, however, a fortune teller told one of the women that they would all be widows before the expedition was over. Her prediction came true.

"Bad Signs in the Weather"

𝕿*he Narváez expedition left Spain* on June 17, 1527, according to the Old Style calendar used by Cabeza de Vaca. Modern calendars make the date ten days later.

The voyage across the Atlantic was uneventful, and, after a passage of almost two months, the ships reached Santo Domingo on the island of Hispanola. They put into port for more than a month while Narváez resupplied the ships, bought horses, and purchased another vessel. His main concern, however, was to find replacements for nearly a fourth of his men. One hundred forty of them refused to sail any farther.

The ships were then ordered to proceed westward to the next island. There, at the port of Santiago, Cuba, they again took on men, horses, and arms.

While in Santiago, Narváez met Vasco Porcallo de Figueroa, the founder of the town of Trinidad on the west tip of the island. Porcallo offered more supplies if Narváez would go to a nearby island and get them. As a result of this meeting, Porcallo's brother signed on as a high-ranking officer in the expedition.

While on the way to the island, Narváez ordered two of the ships to go ahead for the provisions while the others were ordered to anchor in the harbor at Santa Cruz. He placed Cabeza de Vaca in command of one of the ships and assigned the other to Captain Juan Pantoja, a friend who had led a company of cross-bowmen during the ill-fated battle with Cortés.

When the two ships reached the island where the supplies were stored, Pantoja went ashore, leaving Cabeza de Vaca in charge of the ships. Storm clouds soon gathered, and the pilots were anxious to leave because many ships had been wrecked in that harbor. Winds began to whip around, and a boat came with a message urging Cabeza de Vaca to come ashore. At first he refused, believing it was his duty to take care of the ships, but those on shore sent a second frantic message.

By that time the swells had turned into such huge waves that he could persuade only thirty men to get into the smaller boat and go with him. The others promised to come the next day and attend Sunday church services. As he left, Cabeza de Vaca ordered those remaining aboard to drive the ships onto the beach if a storm developed.

Within an hour the wind turned into a scream. Driving sheets of rain whipped across the area. Everyone ran for shelter, but there was no place to escape the fierce wind and torrential rain. Trees bent over to the ground and were uprooted. Houses were flattened or blown away like match sticks. Only by locking arms and walking eight together could the men make any headway against the wind's powerful force.

All night as the hurricane raged, they kept moving, afraid to stay in one place for fear of being hit by things flying through the air. The roaring wind sounded like many voices ringing in their ears. At the height of the storm they heard sounds that have been reported by others who have experienced the full force of a hurricane — they thought they heard the tinkle of little bells and the sound of tambourines and flutes.

Morning brought calm, but destruction was every-where. Grass and leaves had been stripped away. Trees and houses no longer stood.

The men rushed to the shore, but there were no ships in sight. Far down the beach they found the bodies of two sailors dashed on the rocks. One of the ship's small boats was lodged in a tree three-quarters of a mile from the shore. A cloak and quilt, torn to shreds, were all they recovered. The frightening storm claimed the lives of sixty men and twenty horses on the two ships. Cabeza de Vaca sent the king a report of the awesome event.

Not long afterward Narváez arrived with the four remaining ships. Those aboard were so frightened by reports of the storm and the loss of their companions that they persuaded the governor to delay the voyage to Florida until the following spring when the storms would be gone.

During this time of waiting, Narváez took one ship and went to Trinidad to spend the winter. The others were placed under the command of Cabeza de Vaca and ordered to anchor on the south coast of Cuba until the governor returned.

Finally, as spring approached, Narváez arrived in a two-masted brig he had purchased. He brought with him a new pilot who claimed to know the whole coast between Florida and New Spain. Outfitted with five ships, four hundred men, and eighty horses, the flotilla set out on February 22, 1528. Waiting to join them in Havana was another ship with forty infantry and twelve horsemen.

The fleet had barely lifted anchor before the pilot ran the ships aground, and they had to wait fifteen days until storm swells lifted them off the reefs. Then, as they tried to round the west end of Cuba, the wind prevented them from reaching Havana. Storm after storm blocked their way.

Giving up the effort, the five ships sailed northward without their companion ship. The gales blew them toward Florida and the unspeakable woe that awaited them.

"My Honor Would be Impugned"

Running *before the wind,* the Narváez expedition sighted land on Tuesday, April 12, 1528. For the next two days they sailed along the west coast of the Florida peninsula.

Heading into a bay somewhere near SARASOTA, they saw Indian houses. While the ships were anchored in the mouth of the bay, the purser Enríquez went ashore. In a friendly encounter with the Indians, he traded trinkets for fish and venison. The food was a welcome change after six weeks of sea rations.

Three days later, on Good Friday, Narváez took the officials ashore and in a formal ceremony planted a Spanish flag. He read a proclamation stating his credentials as governor and claimed all the land for the King of Spain. Afterwards Cabeza de Vaca and the other officers laid their royal commissions before him, signifying his authority.

By this act, Narváez officially founded a town, not only claiming the land for King Charles V of Spain but declaring everyone living there to be subjects of the crown. The Indian "subjects" were nowhere in sight.

That same day, Cabeza de Vaca led a small group of men into a deserted Indian village. Among the buildings there was one of enormous size, large enough to hold a hundred persons. But the greatest excitement occurred with the discovery of a small gold bell among the fishing nets.

The Spanish had reason to rejoice. There had been no warlike confrontations with the Indians and this small gold object seemed to promise a great future.

The following day, a confident Narváez directed the pilot of the brig to search for a harbor along the coast. If they did not find it, they were to sail to Havana, fill their other ship with provisions, and return.

Then he turned his attention to the land. The forty-two horses that had survived the voyage were brought ashore. Many were weak and almost useless, but the commander set out immediately to investigate the territory he ruled. He took Cabeza de Vaca, the quartermaster Solís, Father Suárez, and six horsemen with him.

Soon they located OLD TAMPA BAY and captured four Indians. By signs, the Spaniards indicated that they wanted corn, and the Indians led them to a village where there was corn growing in the fields, but it was too green to eat.

While there, they saw some crates that looked like the ones Spanish merchants used to ship goods. To their astonishment each crate held a dead body covered with painted deerskin. They also saw pieces of linen, canvas cloth, shoes, some iron, and feather headdresses from New Spain. All these items indicated that the crates had washed ashore from a wrecked ship. The priest, believing the corpses to be idols, ordered them to be burned.

Again the Spaniards found samples of gold. Where, they asked the Indians, could they get more? The Indians pointed northward. At a faraway place called Apalachee, they said, the Spaniards would find all the corn and gold they wanted.

Marching thirty miles farther, the Spaniards found a small village with large corn fields as well as some dried corn. Satisfied with this, they returned to the ships.

Armed with such favorable information, Narváez called a council of the officers. He also included a sailor and the notary whose job it was to record all actions in order for the king to have a true account of events and decisions.

In the meeting Narváez laid out his plan to take a force of soldiers inland. The ships, meanwhile, would move along the coast until they reached the harbor at Pánuco in New Spain. This excellent harbor was near the Río de las Palmas at the western extent of his authority. The pilot assured them that the harbor at Pánuco was not far away, but in fact it was almost a thousand miles away in a straight line across the GULF OF MEXICO and nearly double that if the coastline were followed.

Cabeza de Vaca, knowing that as a senior officer he would be held responsible if something happened to the ships, immediately objected. He argued that they should not leave the ships until they were in a safe harbor. Besides, the horses were too weak, and there was not enough food to provide the soldiers for the march. Further, it was his opinion that the soil where they had landed was too poor to sustain a settlement. He felt that they needed to find a more suitable place before the ships were sent away.

The majority of the group, however, sided with Narváez. The priest even pointed out that they might incur divine wrath if they abandoned the project. Only the notary agreed with Cabeza de Vaca. Finally, it was decided that one hundred passengers, including the women, were to stay with the ships. A force of three hundred men would march along the coast in the direction of "nearby" Pánuco and rendezvous with the ships.

Outnumbered, Cabeza de Vaca asked the notary to draw up a paper stating his objection to abandoning the ships before they were in a safe harbor, a statement he could use in court if the ships were lost. Narváez bristled at this request. He ordered the notary instead to make a statement that they were abandoning their first settlement in favor of a more suitable place.

Then, in front of everyone, he insulted his second in command. Since Cabeza de Vaca was afraid to go into the interior, the governor said, he could take charge of the ships. Cabeza de Vaca, his honor questioned, stalked out of the council.

For two days Narváez sent messages asking him to change his mind. Perhaps he wanted a responsible person in charge of the ships, but it may have been his way of getting rid of an officer who opposed his ideas. Or perhaps he wanted somebody else to have the responsibility if the ships were lost. In any case, Cabeza de Vaca obstinately refused.

When Narváez pressed him for a reason, he replied that regardless of how ill equipped they were for the journey inland, he would run that risk and endure whatever hardships came rather than have it said that he took charge of the ships and stayed behind because of fear. He preferred, he said, to risk his life rather than place his honor in that position.

Narváez then followed through with his plan and sent the ships away under the command of a friend. Their instructions were to sail to a harbor the pilot said was nearby and wait there for the rest of them. The ships followed the coastline but found no harbor. They had already passed TAMPA BAY. Those on the land never saw the ships again.

"A Province Called Apalachee"

On May 1, 1528, three hundred soldiers, each equipped with two pounds of biscuits and one-half pound of bacon, began marching in a northerly direction, Cabeza de Vaca rode with the forty horsemen, but instead of staying close to the coast as originally planned, Narváez headed to the interior. His goal was Apalachee in the area of the Florida panhandle near TALLAHASSEE.

After marching two weeks without seeing any Indian villages, they were desperate for food. The soldiers were so hungry that they ate the stalks of palmetto plants.

Then, some distance farther, they spent a day crossing the Withlacoochee River. Near there, they captured six Indians who led them to some deserted houses where they eagerly devoured the corn.

When Cabeza de Vaca insisted that they find their ships, the governor placed him in charge of a scouting party of forty foot soldiers commanded by Captain Alonso del Castillo. They marched toward the coast but found no harbor where ships could anchor. Narváez continued the journey on toward Apalachee.

Six weeks into their march, on June 17, exactly one year after leaving Spain, they were amazed at the sight of a strange group approaching them. An Indian chief, wearing a painted deerskin cloak, was riding on the back of one of his subjects. He was surrounded by others playing reed flutes. By signs, Narváez found out that they were enemies of the Apalachee tribe. He gave beads and hawk bells to the chief, and in return the chief gave Narváez his painted deerskin.

The Spaniards travelled on with these Indians until they came to the Suwannee River. It was too wide and swift to cross on rafts, so they spent nearly all the next day crossing in a canoe. When an impatient cavalryman tried to swim his horse across, both horse and rider were swept away and drowned. This first loss of life greatly saddened the whole group.

The chief invited the Spaniards to his village and provided corn for them to eat, but that evening an arrow narrowly missed one of the soldiers. When daylight came, the Indians had disappeared. The Spaniards marched away with a rear guard to prevent attack and soon captured several Indians to use as guides.

Their journey led through unusual country. The flat, sandy land was filled with amazingly tall trees, many of which had been blown over in storms or split by lightning. They saw bears, "lions" (panthers), and several kinds of deer, but what interested them most was a small animal with a pocket for carrying its young. They had never seen an opossum. Birds, especially ducks and water birds, were everywhere. Apparently, they did not see any alligators.

Fallen trees and swamps slowed their progress, but finally, on June 24, they approached Apalachee. The gnawing hunger and the shoulders rubbed raw by armor all seemed worth it. Then they saw the town. Instead of palaces filled with gold and food, Apalachee was forty thatched huts, set in low places in the dense forest to protect them from storms.

Narváez ordered Cabeza de Vaca and Solís to take nine horsemen and fifty infantry into the town. They found it deserted except for women and children. A search yielded nothing of value — just a few pieces of painted deerskin, some poorly woven shawls, and several bowls for grinding corn.

Suddenly, the Apalachee warriors returned. They killed Solís's horse, then vanished. Two hours later they returned to ask the release of their women and children, and the Spaniards freed everyone except a chief whom they held as hostage.

The next day the Indians shot flaming arrows into the thatched huts where the Spaniards were staying before fleeing again into the corn fields and swamps. On the third day, the Indian prince Don Pedro fell dead in a hail of arrows.

During the twenty-six days the Spaniards remained in the area, they made three expeditions into the surrounding country. By mid-July, it was clear that Apalachee was the largest village in the area. There was no gold. Bitterly disappointed, they turned toward the seacoast in search of food they so desperately needed. Their destination, a town called Aute, was reported to have corn, beans, melons and fish.

Deadly accurate Indian arrows dogged their steps as they struggled along through swamps choked by fallen trees. The Indians carried bows that were six or seven feet long and as thick as a man's arm. The agile Indians easily pulled the bows and let fly arrows that penetrated trees as thick as a man's leg. Their shots, accurate for a distance of two hundred yards, pierced the Spanish armor.

For eight days the Spaniards were easy targets for Indian arrows as they walked in water up to their armpits. Many, including Cabeza de Vaca, were injured, and several were killed.

Then they reached Aute, and their hearts sank at the sight of the burned, deserted houses. The only bright spot was the fields of squash and beans that were beginning to ripen.

After resting a couple of days, Narváez sent Cabeza de Vaca, Father Suárez, Captain Castillo, and Andrés Dorantes, along with seven horsemen and fifty infantry, to find the sea. During their two-day exploration, they found many inlets and even had a meal of oysters, but they returned with bleak news. They were still a long way from the sea.

On arrival back at the camp, the search party found that their companions had barely survived a nighttime attack by the Indians. Nearly all were ill or injured. There were not enough horses to carry them, but staying in Aute was not an option. If they did not reach the coast, they would all die.

Struggling against starvation, sickness, death, and Indian attacks, they made their way to the sea. Again they came face to face with disappointment. There was no sign of the ships. It would be years before Cabeza de Vaca learned that the ships spent a year searching the coast for them before sailing to New Spain.

For those on shore, the desperate situation led some of the cavalry to plot to take the horses and abandon the others. Narváez, however, discovered the plan and stopped it, but the mutiny shook him badly. He called everyone together to ask each man what he thought they should do.

Everyone agreed that they had to reach Pánuco in order to survive, but they had encountered so many obstacles on land that it seemed better to travel by water. But they had no ships and no one knew how to build any. Even if they had, there were no tools or forge to make tools to construct the boats. There was no oakum or pitch to seal out water if they got them built, and there was no rigging for the sails. Worst of all, there was no food to eat while they were working.

Gloom hung over the camp until one man said he thought he could make a furnace to melt iron. With ingenuity born of desperation, they constructed a make-shift furnace. Soon stirrups, buckles, spurs, and crossbows had been shaped into nails, saws, and axes.

They cut logs to build the flatboats, caulked them with palmetto oakum, and sealed them with pine pitch made by a Greek named Doroteo Teodoro. They used their shirts to make sails and plaited the manes and tails of horses, as well as palmetto fibers, to make rope for rigging. Small trees served as rudders and paddles, but finding stones large enough to use as anchors required diligent searching.

To keep the group from starving, several able-bodied men returned to Aute four times and brought one hundred bushels of corn back to the construction site. Every third day, they killed a horse and ate it, skinning the legs whole to make water bags.

The work which began on August 4 was completed on September 20. Two days later, they killed the last horse and ate a final meal. Then they stepped aboard the five flatboats.

Each one was about thirty feet long and held almost fifty men. On board were beads and bells which could be used to trade with the Indians and parched corn to stave off hunger. Crowded shoulder to shoulder, they pushed off into the waves, trusting their fate to crude boats with sides barely six inches out of the water.

Twelve years later Indians would lead part of Hernando de Soto's forces to a cove on APALACHEE BAY. It was the place the Narváez expedition called *Vaya de Cavallos* (Bay of Horses). Burned-out logs and scattered charcoal marked the place where two hundred forty-two desperate men had done the impossible.

"We Gave to this Island
the Name of Malhado"

𝕿*he strange fleet, so different* from the five ships
Narváez had once commanded, stayed close to the shore.
The governor's boat held forty-nine of the strongest men.
Two others, the one commanded by the purser Enríquez
and Father Suárez and the one commanded by Cabeza
de Vaca and the tax agent Solís, also carried forty-nine
men. Captain Castillo and Andrés Dorantes were in
charge of forty-eight men in the fourth boat. The fifth,

under the command of captains Téllez and Peñalosa, had forty-seven passengers.

For thirty days the boats sailed westward along the coast of the Sea of the North, stopping at inlets in search of food and water. Hunger was always present. When the waterbags made from horses's legs rotted, thirst nearly drove them mad. Five men died from drinking sea water.

As they sailed along, they had little contact with Indians until a storm made them seek shelter on an island for nearly a week. Suddenly they were faced with many canoes. When the Spaniards accepted an invitation to come to their village, they found water and cooked fish stored in jars in front of houses made of woven mats. They exchanged some of their corn for the fish.

The chief took Narváez to his house, but at midnight the Indians made a surprise attack. In the struggle the Spaniards grabbed the chief, but he wriggled free, leaving in their hands an exceptionally beautiful fur cloak.

Narváez was wounded in the fracas but fought his way to the shore. He managed to get to his boat while fifty Spaniards, including Cabeza de Vaca, held the Indians at bay. At dawn when their arrows were gone, the Indians withdrew. In retaliation for the attack, the Spaniards broke up the Indian canoes and used the wood to raise the sides of their boats.

Continuing westward in search of Pánuco, they sailed into MOBILE BAY, desperate for water. When a lone canoe of Indians offered to fill their containers, Teodoro, the one who had showed them how to make pine pitch to seal the boats, volunteered to go with them. The Indians not only returned without the water but also without Teodoro and the servant who went with him. The Greek may have stayed of his own will. The Spaniards never saw him or his servant again, but in 1540 Indians reported to Hernando de Soto that two men had stayed with them for a while before moving on.

The loss of these companions grieved them, but the survivors continued their journey. They explored the mouths of several rivers. When they reached the MISS-ISSIPPI, they were astonished to find that they could dip fresh water from the sea. The current was so strong that when they tried to enter the mouth of the river, they were pushed back into the gulf.

The boats tried to stay near each other, but Narváez had taken the strongest men. As they drifted apart, Cabeza de Vaca asked for a line, but Narváez refused. The situation was so desperate, he said, that each person must do what he felt best for his own safety. Soon the boats lost sight of each other.

Cabeza de Vaca's boat drifted alone, its occupants collapsing from hunger and thirst. By the night of November 5, they were more dead than alive. Only Cabeza de Vaca and his navigator were able to handle the rudder. Around midnight they heard breakers and tried to stay off shore so they would not crash in the dark, but at dawn a huge wave lifted the boat and flung it onto the shore.

The jolt jarred the survivors awake. The men, so starved that their bones showed, lay exhausted on the beach. The strongest, Lope de Oviedo, was sent to climb a tree and from his perch reported that they were on an island. They had reached GALVESTON on the TEXAS coast.

It was not long before they were surrounded by two hundred Indians with painted faces and stalks of cane stuck through their earlobes. To the exhausted Spaniards, the Karankawa Indians looked like giants. Cabeza de Vaca and Solís offered beads and bells and made signs that they needed food. The Indians gave arrows in friendship and the next day brought fish and some underwater roots that tasted like nuts.

Revived, the Spaniards dug their boat out of the sand, stowed their clothing on board, and pushed off into the water. Just after they had scrambled aboard, a huge wave overturned the boat. Solís and two others clung to the boat and drowned when the wreckage sank. The next breaker flung all the others back onto the beach.

In an instant they had lost friends and their only means of escape. They were shivering in the cold wind, lamenting their cruel fate, when the Indians returned. They too sat down and cried loudly for half an hour.

Although the situation was desperate, some in the group were reluctant to go to the Indian village. Having previously been to the New World, they knew that Indians sacrificed their victims. Facing sure death from starvation and exposure, they decided to take the chance.

Since the village was some distance away, the Indians built fires along the path. Then, holding each man so that his feet barely touched the ground, they ran from one fire to the next until they had reached their houses. During the night of loud celebration the Spaniards feared the worst, but peaceful Indians greeted them when morning came.

That same day Cabeza de Vaca was startled to see an Indian wearing a trinket such as they had carried to trade with the Indians, but it was not one he had given away. Then he learned that all forty-eight men aboard the Castillo/Dorantes boat were nearby.

The two groups met, and in their misery named the island Malhado. But as bad as things had been this far, they would get worse. The Isle of Misfortune was aptly named.

"The Time I Spent in This Land"

Still *anxious to leave*, the Spaniards sent four good swimmers and an Indian guide south to find Pánuco. Once there, they would alert the Spanish government to come rescue the rest of them.

Soon after these men left, the others split up between two tribes living on the island. Because the Indians did not farm, they moved around to find food. From October to February they stayed on the island eating fish, supplemented by roots of an underwater plant which was edible during November and December.

36

Following this time, the tribe moved to the mainland. During March and April they lived on oysters gathered along the coast, tossing the shells aside. Over the years great mounds built up, and the Indians pitched their mat houses on these beds of oyster shells. April, the month for celebrations and dances, was a time for fighting mosquitos while gathering blackberries.

The happiest time of the year, however, was the five or six months the Indians feasted on prickly pear cactus. The Indians called it *tuna*, and many tribes came together in central TEXAS to pick the fruit that is about the size of a hen's egg. Nobody went hungry during *tuna* season. The Indians squeezed the juice out of the red and black fruit and drank it. They dried the rest and pounded the broad, flat cactus pads into powder. The season lasted a long time because prickly pear spreads over TEXAS in the area west of the COLORADO River. The Indians moved north and west as the fruit ripened.

When fall came, they returned to the lower COLORADO River to gather pecans. Tribes came from a hundred miles away to eat the sweet meat found in the nuts. The Indians shelled the pecans, which came in bumper crops every other year, and mixed them with a kind of grain. For two months that was all they ate. Then it was time to return to the coast to eat fish and underwater roots.

The Spaniards observed their hosts, noting that they were very kind to their children. They also noted that the women, dressed in cloth woven from the moss that hung from trees, did all the heavy work.

At first the Indians treated the Spaniards well, but when they grew tired of feeding their guests, they sent them to other Indians or drove them out of their camp. During this time Cabeza de Vaca became separated from Castillo and Dorantes. Before long, all the Spaniards were slaves of the Indians.

One day, the captives were shocked when the Indians brought some of their sick and demanded that the Spaniards cure them. They tried to refuse because none of them was trained as a doctor, but the Indians threatened to cut off their food. Faced with this choice, they became healers.

They had observed the Indians curing people by blowing on a stick, and they adapted this method, reciting prayers and making the sign of the cross over the sick Indians. To their astonishment the ones who had been ill stood up and announced they were cured.

About this time a great sickness killed many people, and the Indians blamed the Spaniards, but when they talked of killing them, the Indian who held Cabeza de Vaca stopped them. These men are dying too, he pointed out. Persuaded by these words, they left the men alone although the Spaniards probably had brought the disease. In any case, everyone suffered. Within a short time there were only fifteen survivors from the two boats that had landed on Malhado.

In February 1529 the Indians holding Cabeza de Vaca went to the mainland to eat oysters. Two months later, while gathering blackberries, he became very ill. Meanwhile, Dorantes and Castillo, unable to stand their hard life, rounded up all the survivors and made plans to leave. When Dorantes learned that Cabeza de Vaca was on the mainland, he gave some Indians the beautiful fur robe that the escaping chief had left in their hands many months before. They were to bring Cabeza de Vaca to him, but his friend was too ill to travel. Two others, Lope de Oviedo and the notary Alaniz, who did not have long to live, were also too sick to escape.

Leaving these behind, the others raced south along the coast. On the way, they found the overturned Enríquez/Suárez boat. Continuing on down to Espíritu Santo (MATAGORDA BAY), they found Figueroa, one of the four swimmers sent to Pánuco. None of the swimmers had gotten past that point. Only Figueroa was alive, and he was living with some Indians. It was clear that nobody was coming to rescue them.

During the brief time they were together, Figueroa told them how the occupants of the Enríquez/Suárez boat made it to shore at the mouth of the SAN BERNARD River. Then, as they headed south, Narváez's boat caught sight of them on the banks of Espíritu Santo and ferried them across the bay. After putting his own men ashore, he refused to land himself. That night a wind drove him out to sea, and he was never seen again.

Before his boat disappeared, Narváez had revoked Enríquez's command and given it to his friend, Juan Pantoja. Pantoja was so cruel that the brother of the wealthy Cuban who had helped finance the trip struck Pantoja on the head and killed him. One by one the men had died, and the others roasted their flesh and ate. The one who survived was Hernando de Esquivel. Figueroa heard the story from Esquivel and tried to persuade his comrade to go south with him. Esquivel refused, saying that the priests told him they had already passed Pánuco.

As the men talked, the Indians returned and forced Figueroa to leave with them. He barely had time to tell them which tribe was holding Esquivel.

The escapees from Malhado did not remain free long, but Dorantes, unable to stand the harsh treatment, ran away to the Indians who held Esquivel. They told him the Spaniard had been killed when he tried to escape. They showed Dorantes a book, beads, and the sword that belonged to Esquivel.

During the time the escapees were making their way down the coast, Cabeza de Vaca recovered from his near-fatal illness. When he realized they were gone, he was bitterly disappointed. "I did not even get to see them," he said.

By the spring of 1530, Cabeza de Vaca could stand his cruel treatment no longer. His hands bled from pulling underwater roots and his shoulders were bruised from carrying wood. He had observed that the Indians valued certain things, but these often came from territory controlled by their enemies. And so he began to trade things between tribes.

For several years he moved freely over a wide area of TEXAS. From the coast he went as far north as the RED River with conches and other sea shells that were used for cutting. He also carried beans which the Indians used for medicine and a ceremonial drink. On his return, he brought hides, red ocher for body paint, arrow shafts, flint for arrowheads and the glue and sinew to attach them. He also brought tassels of deer hair which the Indians dyed red.

During his trips he saw many kinds of animals. On three occasions he saw "cattle." The American bison ranged over the GREAT PLAINS all the way southward to central TEXAS. He described them as about the size of Spanish cattle but with brown and black woolly hair and short horns. The meat, he said, was sweeter and tasted better than Spanish beef. The Indians made robes, shoes, and shields from the hides, and perhaps the hides of these animals were among the skins he traded to the coastal Indians.

For the five years he worked as a trader, the only Spaniard he saw was Lope de Oviedo. For some reason the one who had been the strongest when they landed seemed paralyzed by fear. Each year when Cabeza de Vaca came to Malhado, Oviedo promised to leave with him. But when the time came, he backed out because he didn't know how to swim and was afraid to cross rivers.

Finally Cabeza de Vaca succeeded in convincing Oviedo to leave, but when they reached MATAGORDA BAY, they were surrounded by Indians who bragged about killing other Spaniards. To demonstrate, they beat the men and pressed arrow points into their chests. Oviedo, overcome with fear, retreated to Malhado with some women who were going in that direction.

Two days later the Indians holding Castillo and Dorantes came to gather pecans on the lower COLORADO River near its entrance into MATAGORDA BAY. A joyful Cabeza de Vaca went to greet them. Castillo and Dorantes stood speechless, staring at the man they had thought long dead.

As the men talked, pieces of the puzzle concerning the fate of their companions fell into place. Only the Téllez/Peñalosa boat was unaccounted for, and it would be two years before they knew its fate. From this point on, Álvar Núñez Cabeza de Vaca, Alonso del Castillo Maldonado, Andrés Dorantes, and Dorantes's slave Estevánico concentrated their efforts on getting to New Spain.

As desperate as they were to escape, they knew the pecan season was ending. With the weather turning cold, there would be no food along their route. They faced the grim fact that they must wait another year, but as the tribes went their separate ways, the Spaniards had a plan in place. The following summer when the Indians gathered to eat the *tuna*, they would seek freedom.

"Children of the Sun"

For all their careful planning, the four survivors did not leave when the tribes met in central TEXAS in August 1533. Their hopes of escape vanished when the tribes quarreled and went separate ways soon after arriving at the *tuna* fields. For the Spaniards it meant another year of mistreatment, hunger, and waiting to be free.

Then, in 1534, as the season of the prickly pears came once again, the tribes gathered on the rolling hills near SAN ANTONIO to eat the juicy cactus. Three times that year Cabeza de Vaca had been forced to run for his life when the Indians became angry with him. He had made his decision — he would escape this time or die in the attempt.

Quite by accident as the tribes mingled, he learned the fate of the fifth boat that had sailed with them across the GULF OF MEXICO. He was directed to a nearby group of coastal dwellers who showed him clothing and weapons that had belonged to men on the Téllez/Peñalosa barge. The Indians had killed the exhausted Spaniards as they lay on the beach unable to defend themselves.

It was clear now that all five boats that left the Bay of Horses had reached the coast of TEXAS. In the intervening six years, starvation, exposure, and Indian attack had brought death to their companions. Other than Figueroa and Oviedo, whom they never saw again, there was no one else to make the trip to New Spain with them.

The four met briefly while they were in an area close to each other. Because the *tuna* ripened later in the northern regions, their plan was to go in that direction in order to have food as they traveled.

Before they could escape, however, the tribes drifted apart. Cabeza de Vaca, still determined to leave, sent word to the others. He would leave when the moon was full, whether the others went with him or not.

As the time neared, Dorantes and Estevánico managed to reach him. Then, the next day quite by chance, they moved near the group who held Castillo. As the full moon appeared on September 22, 1534, the four stole away.

All that day, they raced northward. Fear sped them on, and they covered nearly thirty miles, reaching perhaps as far as the GUADALUPE River.

Toward sunset they saw smoke from cooking fires and hurried toward them, but the Indian who spotted them ran away. Estevánico caught up with him and learned where the houses were.

These Indians, ones Cabeza de Vaca called Avavares, came down to trade during the prickly pear season. They spoke a different language from the other Indians, but they had heard of the cures the Spaniards performed and welcomed the runaways. Dorantes and Estevánico were escorted to the house of a shaman, while Castillo and Cabeza de Vaca received the same royal treatment.

That night many Indians appeared. They complained of terrible headaches, and Castillo said the usual prayer. Immediately, the Indians reported that their headaches were gone. To show their appreciation, the Indians brought prickly pears and chunks of venison, which the Spaniards devoured.

These Indians had a good supply of meat. Although they had no horses, the plains Indians were marvelous runners who could tire out the animals they were chasing. Sometimes, they deliberately set prairie fires to drive the animals into areas where they could catch them.

The Avavares spent three days in a great celebration before going farther north to pick prickly pears. It was a hard journey with little food, but as soon as they reached the LLANO River, they found cactus that was still good to eat.

The brush country through which they moved was filled with mesquite, scrub oaks, and rattlesnakes. When the group went to collect beans from the mesquite trees, Cabeza de Vaca lost his way back to camp.

By some miracle he found a bush on fire. For five cold October nights he kept warm by digging a pit to sleep in, dragging up brush, and building fires at the four corners of the sleeping pit. As he travelled each day, he carried a burning torch and enough wood for the night's fire. His only blanket was the straw with which he covered himself. The warming fires worked well except for the night a spark set the straw on fire and singed his hair before he could put it out.

For nearly a week Cabeza de Vaca continued his lonely trek across the lower TEXAS plains. On the sixth day, he stumbled into the camp of his friends. They rejoiced to see him because they assumed that he had died of a rattlesnake bite. Together they shared a meal of prickly pears.

The next morning five sick Indians surrounded by their friends came to ask healing for their stomach cramps. Castillo again said prayers, and the Indians again announced that they were cured. This news brought even more Indians to be healed. Castillo became frightened because he knew there was no real cure in what he was doing. If the "cures" stopped, the Indians might become angry enough to kill them, so he refused to do any more healing.

The Indians immediately turned to Cabeza de Vaca, whom they recognized from his trading days. They asked him to come to their village and heal a man. When he, Dorantes, and Estevánico arrived, many people were in a stupor. The man he was supposed to heal had been given up for dead, and, according to custom, the Indians had knocked down his house and were preparing to burn it.

Cabeza de Vaca examined the man. His eyes were rolled back in his head, and he had no pulse. In spite of the seemingly hopeless situation, the Spaniard did the usual thing. Later that night word came that the man had recovered.

The grateful Indians brought gifts of prickly pears and valuable flint knives. With the *tuna* nearly gone, it seemed best to stay with the Avavares for the winter.

During the cold nights, the Indians told about a creature they called *Mala Cosa* (Bad Thing), who had suddenly appeared among them sixteen years earlier.

Bad Thing never showed his face completely. He would appear at their door with a burning torch, grab a victim, cut out part of his intestines, then throw it into the fire. Sometimes he came to their dances and at other times lifted up their houses and let them crash back to earth. The Indians tried to appease him, but he never spoke a word nor ate any of the food they offered. It seemed a fanciful story to the Spaniards, but the fearful Indians showed them scars from the cuts Bad Thing had made.

That winter brought suffering to everyone as they all struggled to find something to eat. Cold weather had driven the animals away, and without crops to harvest, the Avavares knew winter as a time of gnawing hunger.

During early summer of 1535, Cabeza de Vaca and Estevánico slipped off to some Indians a day's journey away. Estevánico proved his worth as an interpreter. While the others felt it was better to stay aloof, Estevánico did not. He mingled freely with the Indians, and by the time they returned to Mexico City, he could speak five different Indian languages.

After the other two Spaniards joined them, they went with the Indians to eat the fruit of some small trees, perhaps persimmons. Their hunger became so great that they ate the *tuna* while it was still green. The milky liquid burned their mouths and made them even thirstier. Adding to their misery, the broiling sun blistered them so badly they shed their skins like snakes.

These Indians gave their visitors no preferential treatment, and their hunger was worse than ever. They carried wood and water and dug roots. Cabeza de Vaca gladly took the job of scraping animal skins because he could eat the scraps. The four quickly learned to eat their food raw before someone took it from them.

In desperation, Cabeza de Vaca turned again to trading. The Indians spent so much time looking for food that they had no time to make things they needed. He taught his companions to make bows, arrows, nets, and combs. He showed them how to make mats like those the Indians used for houses. All of these were traded for food.

One day the Spaniards traded some nets for two dogs. Gulping down this food, they hurried away.

They walked all day in driving rain, and it was not long before they lost the trail. At last they found some green cactus in an area of scrubby trees and made an oven to bake the prickly pears overnight. By morning the *tuna* was edible, and when daylight come, they found the trail again.

At nightfall they reached a village of fifty houses. The Indians, fascinated by the beards, rubbed their hands over the Spaniards' faces and then felt of their own smooth faces.

Soon after leaving these Indians, some women begged the men to follow them home, but the Spaniards were too impatient to wait for the women to rest.

Leaving immediately over an unmarked trail, they soon became lost. After about twelve miles, they came to BIG SPRING, a mammoth spring in central west TEXAS. To their surprise they found the women waiting there.

The women led them to the CONCHO River, which was chest deep from August rains. At a village of one hundred houses, the Indians greeted them with fierce yells and slapped their hands on their thighs.

The food changed as the country changed. At one place the Indians made "flour" from the bitter beans growing in long pods on mesquite trees. Beans, hulls and all, were placed in a deep hole and pounded with a thick log about nine feet long. Dirt was added a little at a time until the official taster pronounced it good enough to eat. Then everyone reached in and took a handful. The mixture of beans, dirt, and water made their stomachs swell but relieved the hunger.

As the survivors traveled through WEST TEXAS, they observed that the Indians had keen senses of hearing and sight and were agile enough to dodge arrows. Some Indians smoked themselves senseless with peyote, a hallucinogen made from a mushroom-shaped, spineless species of cactus. One group was well-built and mild-mannered, but all were blind in one or both eyes.

In another tribe the men made an intoxicating yellow tea from the berries of a holly-like plant. When the drink was ready, the women froze in position when the men called out, "Who wants to drink?" If they moved, the men threw out the tea, believing an evil spirit was in it. During the three days they drank the tea, the men ate nothing.

As news of the healings continued to spread, sick Indians arrived daily to be healed. At one place a great crowd crushed in on the Spaniards until they could hardly breathe. Their hosts rescued them, picking them up so that their feet barely touched the ground, and carried them to the safety of special huts that had been prepared for them. The singing and dancing went on all night, but the Spaniards dared not come out for fear of being suffocated.

Gifts poured in. At one place, the Spaniards received beads, ocher, and little bags of "silver" that was probably mica. At another they were given bows, arrows, and shoes.

Guides from one village led them to the next one before returning home. When the Spaniards received gifts, they took only what they needed and gave the rest to their guides. At one point the guides began to take everything in the village, and the Spaniards were unable to stop the looting. Do not worry, the guides told those being robbed, you will get replacements for your lost possessions at the next village.

Soon, they could see the DAVIS Mountains in the distance. The Spaniards knew that at some point they must turn south to reach New Spain. The Indians told them about an easy, well-watered trail leading through the mountains, but they refused to take it. They understood from the Indians that they were only about fifty miles from the coast, and they had suffered too much misery there. They observed the southeast course of the PECOS River. As long as the rivers flowed toward Malhado, they would not go that way.

Instead, they turned to follow the PECOS north. The trail ran beside the river, but the women guides carried water because, in this part, the river is so salty that it cannot be used for drinking.

Before long, they met some women coming down the trail carrying maize. This crop, which is grown at the great pueblos in central NEW MEXICO, was traded as far south as MEXICO. The Spaniards were overjoyed to find the corn.

Suddenly, the guides turned back down the trail because their enemies lived in the next village. By sunset the Spaniards reached a village of twenty huts, where the inhabitants, aware of the looting, were glad to see them alone. The next day, however, the guides returned and took everything. When the villagers began to weep, the guides stopped them. These men are children of the sun, they said, and you must do what they say.

As the four moved along, they came to a village where the shaman gave them two gourds. The gourds grew many miles away in the upper reaches of the PECOS and RIO GRANDE rivers and floated down during the flood season. The Indians believed the gourds had been sent from heaven and traded items to get them.

These particular gourd rattles had pebbles inside, and they were decorated with two bells and a red and white feather. The Indians used the gourds in ceremonies, and the person who had the gourd held great authority over the others. The Indians presented the rattles to the men they believed were gods.

The Spaniards carried the gourds with them. They had no way of knowing that one of the gourd rattles would be the cause of Estevánico's death four years later.

"Thunderstruck to See Me"

Passing *just east* of Carlsbad Caverns, the group followed the Pecos River as it ascended the high plains. Food, especially game such as antelope, was plentiful. Soon they reached a village with forty lodges. Here the Indians gave Dorantes a large copper rattle with a face on it. The Spaniards marveled at the skill of the metalworkers who had crafted it but were unable to learn where the rattle had come from.

After traveling a good distance up the Pecos, they turned west to follow the Peñasco. While climbing through a pass in the mountains, Cabeza de Vaca thought he saw slag from iron smelting. It was probably iron ore deposits or pitted limestone rocks.

Once they crossed the mountain, the scenery dramatically changed as they came into the area of Cloudcroft, New Mexico. Tall aspens grew on the mountain sides and along the beautiful little river.

The Indians wore cotton shawls and gave the visitors buffalo robes and bags of powdered mica and metallic ore that they used to paint their faces. Mothers brought their children out to see the Spaniards.

Here in the Sacramento Mountains, they added a new food to their diet. They tasted piñon nuts for the first time. The sweet, nutritious seeds grow in tiny cones on the piñon pine and contain an astounding number of calories. For meat the Indians hunted rabbits by surrounding the animal and throwing sticks at it. They also ate venison, and the women brought spiders and worms. The Spaniards had to bless all the food before the Indians would eat it.

A man came to Cabeza de Vaca complaining of the pain caused by an arrow point lodged in his shoulder. Using a sharp flint knife, Cabeza de Vaca removed the enormous arrow point and sewed the wound together with a needle made from a deer bone. The next day the grateful man declared that he was well.

Since the rivers in this region flowed away from Malhado, the Spaniards assumed they had crossed the continental divide and asked to go south. The Indians were reluctant to go that direction because they knew it would be a tortuous journey. Finally persuaded, they began a three-week trek through rough desert, travelling through the foothills to find the few watering places. Gleaming white sands as well as jet-black lava fields lay to the west.

After the long march south, they passed through the GUADALUPE and HUECO mountains and camped near EL PASO. Castillo and Estevánico, accompanied by two women, went into the village. One of the women was a member of the Jumano tribe that lived here on the banks of the RIO GRANDE River. Soon Castillo returned with squashes grown by the inhabitants. Estevánico then led the people out to greet them.

The Indians supplied gourds for carrying water, and they shared buffalo robes with the Spaniards. Because they hunted bison, Cabeza de Vaca called them the Cow People. He considered them the most intelligent of the ones he had met so far.

Even so, they had not learned to make pottery as the pueblo Indians had. In order to cook food, they filled a gourd with water and dropped in heated rocks, replacing them as they cooled. Once the water was hot, food was dropped into the steaming gourd and heated until cooked.

57

It was now November 1535, and again the Spaniards could have turned south and easily reached their destination. But the Rio Grande River flowed toward the coast, and they had no wish to return there.

When the Spaniards stated that they wanted to go toward the sunset, the Indians warned that they would find neither people nor food in that direction. So the Spaniards turned north again and walked beside the Rio Grande.

After seventeen days, they arrived at the Rincon ford and crossed the river there. Then they proceeded north to a creek. For seventeen more days they trudged over Indian trails through mountainous desert, eating only the deer tallow they carried. The Indians ate a juniper berry called *chacan*, but the Spaniards could not stand its bitter taste.

Their fame continued to grow, and now when the Spaniards approached, the Indians piled all their possessions in the middle of the floor of their huts and sat facing the wall with their hair pulled down over their eyes. The Spaniards as usual took what they needed and gave the rest to their guides.

Finally crossing the continental divide somewhere in the area Silver City, New Mexico, they wound their way through mountain passes to the Gila River near the New Mexico-Arizona border.

Walking south, they followed the mountains close to San Simeon, Arizona, past the Chiricahua Mountains, to the area of Douglas, Arizona. Here they crossed into Mexico.

At this point the Spaniards encountered the most civilized Indians they had seen. The Opate Indians had permanent houses. They made good cotton blankets and raised squashes, beans, and maize. The Spaniards, thankful they were again in a land of abundance, loaded these gifts on their guides and sent them home.

Leaving there, the four followed guides on a long journey of more than two hundred miles to the area occupied by the Pima Indians. The land, though mountainous, was fertile, and there was abundant food.

The Pimas gave the Spaniards deer hides as well as excellent cotton blankets they had made. They carried on an extensive trade with areas that were hundreds of miles away. Among the gifts they presented to the Spaniards were beads made from Pacific Ocean coral and fine turquoises from the north.

They had in their possession five "emerald" (probably malachite) arrow points that they valued highly and used in ceremonies and dances. They gave the "emeralds" to Dorantes and explained that the stones had come from far away in the north. To get them they had traded parrot feathers and plumes that had come from southern Mexico.

At a place near Ures, the inhabitants cut open six hundred deer hearts for the travellers. They named the place *Pueblo de los Corazones* (the Town of Hearts). It was here they observed Indians putting the poisonous sap of a small tree on the tips of their arrows.

The trail south led through a fifteen-mile canyon on the Sonora River. Then they left the Sonora and crossed mountains to the Yaqui River, but they had to wait for fifteen days for flood waters to recede.

At a place about thirty miles farther down the river, Castillo stopped in his tracks. An Indian was wearing a peculiar necklace made from a Spanish sword buckle. A horseshoe nail was stitched to it. Other Spaniards had been in this area!

In spite of their excitement at finding traces of the civilization they had left so long ago, the men tried to appear casual. Where, they asked, had these objects come from? The Indians replied that several men, with beards such as they had, had come on horses and killed two of their people. This unsettling news meant that the Indians had encountered slavers, not an exploration party.

Cautiously, for fear the Indians might take out their anger on them, the Spaniards asked what had happened to the men. The Indians answered that they had followed the bearded ones to the coast and watched as they put spears (oars) into the sea. The last they saw of the Spaniards they were moving on top of the waves, going toward the sunset.

As the men continued their journey, they saw other evidence of the slavers. Fertile fields lay empty because the Indians had fled their homes to escape being captured.

Cabeza de Vaca staunchly opposed mistreatment of the Indians and was outraged by this violation of the law. "Clearly," he wrote the king after returning to Spain, "to bring these people to Christianity and subjection to Your Imperial Majesty, they must be won by kindness, the only certain way."

Still walking south, they reached the Río PETATLÁN, now known as the SINALOA River. All along the way the Spaniards saw evidence of many kinds of metal, including gold, antimony, copper, and iron.

More important to them, they saw the tracks and abandoned camping places of their countrymen. Some Indians reported seeing many Indians marching along in chains, and this frightened the others so badly that it was all the Spaniards could do to persuaded them not to run away.

Two days later they found stakes where horses had been tied. With their countrymen so near, Cabeza de Vaca expected the two younger men to go find them, but they refused, saying they were too tired.

Cabeza de Vaca let no such feelings stop him. Anxious to end his long, difficult time away from the civilization, he set out with Estevánico and eleven Indians. Before long they came upon a number of horsemen. The speechless soldiers stared at their long-lost countryman.

When he asked for their leader, they took him to Diego de Alcaraz, the cruel commander in charge of the slave operation. Cabeza de Vaca asked for a certificate showing the year, month, and day that he had arrived. Alcaraz recorded it as March 1536. Dates were not important to the commander, who was upset over the lack of food and Indians. This provoked Cabeza de Vaca to angry words over the way the Indians were being treated.

When Alcaraz learned that many of them were with Cabeza de Vaca's group, he convinced Cabeza de Vaca to call those in hiding to come back to their homes. He promised not to bother them if they would return and bring food. It was a trap. Alcaraz sent the four survivors to Mexico City by a route that was intended to cause their deaths. As soon as they left, the slavers went to work again.

In spite of the deception, the four men reached the outskirts of San Miguel de Culiacán on April 1, 1536. They waited while someone went into town to tell the chief officer that the survivors of the Narváez expedition had arrived.

The mayor hurried out to greet them and stood joyously weeping with them over their return. After hearing about Alcaraz's actions, he called the slaver to Culiacán to answer charges.

The four men spent several weeks in Culiacán before starting on the nine-hundred-mile journey to

Mexico City. There was unrest in the country because of the ill-treatment the Indians had received, and the men were forced to wait for a convoy going in that direction.

From Culiacán they reached Compostela in the province of New Galicia. The governor of this province just north of New Spain was Nuño de Guzmán. Guzmán would be imprisoned and replaced by Coronado the following year because of his cruel treatment of Indians.

In the meantime, however, Governor Guzmán gave his guests a warm reception. He sent proper clothing to wear, but the men found the hot, scratchy clothing painful against their skin. He provided good places for them to stay, but they had forgotten soft beds. Cabeza de Vaca slept on the floor.

Finally, riding on horses provided by Guzmán, they reached Mexico City on Sunday, July 24, 1536. The Viceroy, Antonio de Mendoza, and the conqueror Cortés received them with great honor and ceremony.

The next day was set aside for a *fiesta* and bullfight in their honor. It was the last celebration that Cabeza de Vaca would ever enjoy.

SOUTH AMERICA

Route of Cabeza de Vaca

"Viceroy of the Río de la Plata"

Mexico *City held no interest* for Cabeza de Vaca, but his immediate departure for home was delayed by storms. It was the next spring before he sailed on an uneventful crossing of the Atlantic, Suddenly, however, as they reached the coast of Portugal, a French vessel began to chase them. Only the arrival of Portuguese ships allowed them to escape with the gold and silver they carried. In August 1537 Cabeza de Vaca stepped back onto the soil of his native land, a very different man from the one who had left ten years earlier.

He wasted no time in writing to the king. Convinced he could be successful where Narváez had failed, he sought appointment as governor of Florida. But it was too late. The king had already granted Florida to Hernando de Soto, the brother-in-law of Vasco Núñez de Balboa, discoverer of the Pacific Ocean.

Two of Cabeza de Vaca's kinsmen were going to Florida, and they arranged a meeting with the expedition commander. Hernando de Soto asked the aging conquistador to serve as his second in command, but no agreement was reached. Cabeza de Vaca, perhaps haunted by experiences when he was not in charge, was not aboard when the ships sailed.

Instead, he mounted his horse and went to see the king. Everywhere, people whispered about what he had found in the lands beyond the sea, and the rumors multiplied when he brushed aside their questions. His words were for the king's ears only, he told them, but that only made them believe more strongly that he had found more gold than anyone could count.

Two years passed. Although Spain controlled the lower half of the North American continent and much of South America, there was no suitable position of honor available.

The southern part of the Western Hemisphere had been divided along a boundary set by Pope Alexander VI in 1493. Brazil, east of the line, belonged to Portugal, while Spain got most of the South American continent. Pizarro had already conquered the Incas on the western side, but in the eastern part there were only two settlements. One was Buenos Aires, on the shores of the Río de la Plata. The other was Asunción, farther inland on the Paraguay River.

The Río de la Plata had been discovered by Juan de Solís in 1516, some twenty years earlier. Solís was killed by the Indians, but in Spain the rumor persisted that five of his men had survived and found a land of fabulous wealth.

Ten years after the discovery of the Río de la Plata, Sebastian Cabot, sailing for Spain, explored the broad estuary. Convinced that it came from a place that was rich in silver, he called it Río de la Plata (the Silver River).

In 1535, the year Cabeza de Vaca and his three companions were on their long journey across the American Southwest, Don Pedro de Mendoza, a member of the Spanish royal family, set out for South America with a fleet of fourteen ships. Many of the fifteen hundred men he recruited were high-born noblemen with their families, eager to find fortune in the New World.

They founded the city of Buenos Aires near where the Paraná and Uruguay rivers flow into the Río de la Plata. From the beginning the colony struggled against starvation and Indian attack, and the inept Mendoza sailed for Spain to seek help. Already ill, he died on the way.

Before he left, Mendoza had placed Juan de Ayolas in charge. As soon as Mendoza left, Ayolas set out to explore the Paraná River. Far up the Paraná, in a wilderness where forty-foot red-and-black snakes dragged men under water, he reached the Paraguay River. Farther up that river, he spent six months at a village of cannibals who wore stones in their lips. He called the spot Asunción.

During this time, Ayolas met a Spanish-speaking Indian who claimed to have been a guide for the Solís expedition. Sensing that a fabulous treasure was near, he continued up the Paraguay. At a place he called Candelaria, he left the river and turned west toward the Andes Mountains.

Before departing, he placed Domingo Martínez de Irala in charge of the ships. Irala had orders to wait there to carry the treasure back down the river. After six months the ships began to fall apart. The Indians, painted blue from neck to knees, seemed even more threatening after they refused to bring any food. With his men starving, Irala sailed away. Ayolas had no way to leave when he returned. The Indians lured his group into a swamp and slew them.

Although Irala twice returned to Candelaria to try to find Ayolas, he eventually returned to Asunción and settled there. His strong personality made him a natural leader, and the commission he held from Ayolas placed him in charge of the settlement.

In September 1539, while Cabeza de Vaca waited for word from the king, a ship appeared in the harbor at Seville, Spain. It brought news that the Spanish settlements in Río de la Plata were near starvation. The colonists asked the king for supplies and requested a governor since Mendoza was dead and they did not know what had happened to Ayolas.

Cabeza de Vaca was ready when the Council of the Indies called him to stand before them. With proper ceremony they conferred on him the title Viceroy of the Río de la Plata. The area he ruled stretched east from the Andes to the Atlantic Ocean and south from Brazil to the tip of the continent.

It was the king's policy to spend no money on expeditions. Cabeza de Vaca, wealthy enough to outfit the ships, stood ready to do the king's bidding.

On March 18, 1540, the patent was issued. Its terms, noting Álvar Núñez Cabeza de Vaca's willingness to spend 8,000 ducats plus the cost of transportation, proclaimed him *adelantado*, governor, captain general and chief justice of the province. In effect he not only controlled the military, he was both judge and jury in civil cases. The titles were his, provided the missing lieutenant governor Ayolas was really dead.

In addition to an annual salary of 2,000 ducats, he would receive one-twelfth of the revenues of the province. If he managed to capture a wealthy Indian ruler, he could keep one-sixth of the ransom, after setting aside the King's Fifth. (One-fifth of all treasure was reserved for the king before any divisions were made.)

The document carefully set forth the humane treatment of any natives that were encountered. By King Charles V's decree, all his subjects were to be treated with kindness, and it was Cabeza de Vaca's intention to carry out that policy.

In response to Cabeza de Vaca's request, the patent permitted no lawyers to enter the colony for ten years from its date.

On the steps of the cathedral in Seville, men gathered to request passage with Cabeza de Vaca. Among them was his cousin Pedro Estopiñán Cabeza de Vaca, known as Pero Vaca. The list also included many noblemen, a Flemish drummer, several slaves, four negroes, two Indians (one of them from MEXICO), and six women.

Every man supplied his own sword and dagger, but Cabeza de Vaca provided each with a double set of arms and ammunition. He purchased iron, woolen and linen cloth, ship biscuit, flour, wine, oil, vinegar, and medicines. Trade goods included fish-hooks, knives, mirrors, scissors, red caps, shirts, and shawls. Perhaps remembering the disaster in Florida, he brought an anvil. There were thirty-six sturdy horses, but the ten cows would not survive. In all, he spent 14,000 ducats on supplies, plus 9,000 more on the ships. This exhausted his resources, and he ran up a debt of 5,000 ducats.

In October 1540, following months of preparation, Cabeza de Vaca put on his velvet suit and armor. After mass at the cathedral, he bade his wife goodbye for a second time.

In spite of the careful words the king chose for the patent and the precautions Cabeza de Vaca took, the trip to the Silver River would be even more disastrous than anything he endured in North America.

"We Arrived at Asunción"

$\mathfrak{T}$*he voyage was troubled* from the start. The ships were scarcely out of the harbor before a storm forced them to seek shelter at Cadiz.

It was December before they got under way to the Canary Islands, where an incident occurred that became one of the charges brought against Cabeza de Vaca at his trial. Some soldiers killed three hogs that belonged to the islanders. As punishment, he took their cloaks. The three were the first in a long list of enemies Cabeza de Vaca made in his determination to be fair.

By mid-January they had reached the Cape Verde Islands. During their stay, the leaking flagship was repaired and the horses exercised. Needing supplies, Cabeza de Vaca bought wine, flour, and almonds from one of the ships in the harbor. Another hospitable captain gave him wine and oil. Three years later this courteous act would be turned into a charge of piracy against the Cabeza de Vaca.

Resuming their journey in February, the ships sailed across the Atlantic, meeting each morning and sunset to receive orders.

Their first landfall was in an area controlled by the Portuguese. After resupplying their water barrels, the ships turned south and sailed along the coast until they had crossed the line dividing Portuguese and Spanish territory.

At about longitude forty-eight, they came ashore. Following the custom, Cabeza de Vaca took possession of the land in the name of the king. At his trial three years later, he would be accused of taking possession in his own name and of setting up a stone that had the head of a cow engraved on it.

The fleet did not stay long but sailed two hundred miles farther south. Striking land at Santa Catalina (now called SANTA CATARINA) Island on March 29, 1541, they ended the four-month trip from Cadiz.

Before long a lone ship arrived from Buenos Aires. Nine survivors brought the news that Ayolas was dead. By order of the king, Cabeza de Vaca was governor of a quarter of the South American continent.

After learning that Irala was in the upper country at Asunción, he made the decision to go overland to get there. He felt this route would take less time because the trip by water would have consumed the better part of a year. The water route required a long journey to the Río de la Plata, then tortuous navigation up the Paraná and Paraguay rivers.

The plan to go overland brought objections from those who faced the hardship of walking through wilderness, but the commander who had lived through things they could only imagine was not intimidated.

After determining that there would be tribes along the way to provide food, he placed his cousin, Pero Vaca, in charge of a ship carrying the women and forty men to Buenos Aires. Trade goods were stored in the hold of the flagship, but marchers carried iron for the forge which Cabeza de Vaca insisted on bringing. Along the way, it would be used to turn out chisels, hatchets, fishhooks, and needles while curious Indians watched.

On October 18, 1541, two hundred fifty men, twenty-six of them mounted on horses, along with two priests, were put ashore. Then, with Indians carrying their goods, they started inland. On an impulse Cabeza de Vaca stopped and removed his shoes. He walked the rest of the way barefoot in an effort to inspire his troops. Instead, it brought ridicule.

After nineteen days they reached Guaraní Indians, a tribe that was scattered throughout South America. The Guaranís became allies of the Spaniards, but they had the disturbing habit of eating human flesh, both friend and foe. Cabeza de Vaca was careful to pay in full for the food his men consumed.

His own men caused the most trouble, and he forbade them to pitch their tents near the Indians. This action later led to the charge that he had a monopoly on the food the Indians brought and got rich selling it to the soldiers at a very high price. The Indians, meanwhile, seeing that they were safe, brought their wives and children to see the Spaniards and their horses.

The marchers struggled over steep mountains, across rivers, and through lush jungles where screeching monkeys threw down nuts for the wild boars to eat. After traveling a great arc through the province that Cabeza de Vaca named Vera in honor of his father, they came to the Iguazú river. With great effort they carried their equipment around the magnificent falls, whose roar could be heard twelve miles away.

At the place where the Iguazú and Paraná rivers meet, they were threatened by Indians with feather helmets and bodies painted in many colors. Cabeza de Vaca, arming himself with fascinating objects, walked out to greet them and won over the chief.

At this point on the river Cabeza de Vaca, unaware that Asunción was six hundred miles away, had expected Irala to meet him with boats so that those who were sick could be carried to Asunción. There were no boats. The helpful Indians, using the canoes that had been lashed together to carry the horses across the river, ferried those who were ill downstream to meet Irala's boats.

Meanwhile the main party headed directly west over the rolling plains, and on March 11, 1542, "it pleased God . . . we arrived at the city of Asunción." The journey had taken four months and nine days. A month later the boats arrived with those who had been ill. For all the hardships, only two men had been lost, one drowned in the swirling Paraná River and another killed by a tiger. The daring cross-country gamble had paid off.

Irala greeted the new governor with all the usual formality. He knelt and received the king's decree. Observing the signature, he kissed the paper, touched it to his head, and gave his word to obey. Then the notary read aloud the ordinance that made Cabeza de Vaca governor of the Río de la Plata.

Arriving was one thing, but governing proved to be another. Three hundred fifty citizens of Asunción heard the decree, but many were not anxious to follow the new leader. With their own hands they had created the little town of thatch-roofed wooden buildings, and they wanted no interference from an outsider. Irala was their leader.

Cabeza de Vaca began immediate changes that were not popular. After finding that the wealth was in the hands of a few persons, he wiped out all debts, saying he would pay them if the Council of the Indies did not. This relieved the poor, but angered the rich. Food supplies were adequate, but clothing was very scarce. The governor used his own supplies to provide clothing and guns for those who had no money. He found that taxes had been collected but was incensed to learn that the tax collectors had taken an equal amount for themselves.

For some unexplained reason he also forbade anyone to buy wildcats or parrots without his consent.

The use of Guaraní Indians as servants proved to be the biggest problem. These Indians, except for their disturbing habit of eating human flesh, were peaceful. They raised geese and kept parrots in their houses. They grew corn, beans, pumpkins, yams, and peanuts. In addition, they supplied the Spaniards with fish from the rivers and wild turkeys from the forest. They made excellent bread from manioc (cassava root) and concocted a stimulating tea called *yerbe maté* and a fermented drink called *chicha*.

It disturbed Cabeza de Vaca to see the Guaranís treated as slaves, and he immediately ordered that the king's decree concerning their freedom be read aloud for everyone to hear. Irala, who had many Guaranís in his service, was one of those affected.

To bring some control, the new governor ordered a curfew. The Guaranís could leave their village and visit their relatives in town, but no Spaniard could leave the town without his permission. He also forbade the sale of slaves, but this left the Guaranís unable to sell their own slaves, so they ate them.

Distrustful of the notary who had served Irala, he gave that position to Pedro Hernández, one of the founders of Buenos Aires. This embittered the deposed notary, but he would get the last say when he delivered many charges against the governor at his trial in Spain.

Cabeza de Vaca solved the problem of the very popular Irala by appointing him as second in command. Irala accepted the assignment.

In order to set what he thought was a good example for his colonists, the governor lived an austere life. He did not miss a single day of going to mass, and he supplied vestments, flour and a barrel of wine for the sacraments. He worked with his own hands to help build the new church, Our Lady of September.

His attitude toward the Indians was one of pacification, and he followed it whenever possible. However, when a tribe molested the Guaranís, he sent a force against them. Then, to everyone's astonishment, he pardoned the enemy captives after they promised to be loyal to the king of Spain. This policy was a great success. Each week on market day these Indians brought two hundred canoes filled with food.

There was no gold in Asunción, but rumors placed fabulous wealth somewhere to the west. Cabeza de Vaca sent Irala up the river with orders to find a way to get there. While waiting for Irala to return, Cabeza de Vaca sent a ship to Buenos Aires. It returned with all the remaining citizens, and the city would not be resettled for another forty years.

Less than a year after he came to Asunción, a terrible fire burned most of the city. To prevent that again, Cabeza de Vaca ordered that new buildings be made of clay. Then he had large tree trunks sunk six feet into the ground to form a wall around the town. In the center of the area, they built a fort.

Irala returned a week after the fire. He had gone far up the river and found a tribe of Indians who had been to the mountains in the west. He himself had taken a three-day journey in that direction and had information about the fabulous cities there.

On the way home, he had carried out Cabeza de Vaca's order to execute a treasonous Indian chief, and this had angered the tribes in the area. There was unrest all around, and as required by law, Cabeza de Vaca assembled the officials and priests. All voted to punish the Indians, but when the chief offenders were captured, they asked for peace, and Cabeza de Vaca granted it.

With everything peaceful, Cabeza de Vaca was ready to search for the fabled Gilded Man. According to stories, this king beyond the Andes was sprinkled with gold dust every day and then washed in a lake. Pizarro had found such wealth in Peru, and Cabeza de Vaca expected to do the same. In addition, the road he established would cross the continent and eliminate the dangerous passage through the Strait of Magellan to reach the Pacific Ocean.

Always a loner, Cabeza de Vaca had few friends. When he left Asunción in search of the Gilded Man, he placed one of these, Juan de Salazar de Espinosa, in charge of the defence of the city.

He took known troublemakers with him, and their opposition doomed the expedition.

"On the Ground of a Sufficient Number of Witnesses"

*O**n September 8, 1543*, four hundred Spaniards entered ten boats for the trip up the Paraguay River. Accompanying them were one hundred twenty canoes which carried ten Guaranís each. Ten mounted soldiers rode along the tree-lined shore until the way was no longer passable. Food was plentiful, and everything proceeded smoothly as they set out in search of treasure.

Cabeza de Vaca stopped often to talk with the Indians. At one place he met a chief who said that his tribe had killed the explorer Ayolas. He claimed to know the hiding place of the sixty loads of silver that Ayolas had brought over the Andes, but the next day the Indians vanished. The treasure was never found.

Brushing this disappointment aside, the expedition moved on up the river. The pleasant countryside turned into a flat area with twisting rivers running through foul-smelling marshes. Rattlesnakes, lizards, caymans, tarantulas, and paralyzing wasps greeted them. Armadillos, monkeys, deer, opossums, and sloths were everywhere. Macaws and gray-throated green parakeets built nests six feet across. Anteaters feasted at ant hills higher than a man seated on a horse. Amid all this, a bat left the sleeping governor with a bloody toe.

One month after they started, the expedition reached the limit of Irala's earlier exploration near Lake Gaiba. Here they found eight hundred lodges of Indians the Spaniards called "Great Ears" because their ear lobes had been stretched so much that they hung down to their shoulders. During battle, they tied the lobes in a knot behind their heads. These people slept in hammocks and kept ducks to eat the crickets in their houses.

On November 26, 1543, after spending two weeks with the "Great Ears," Cabeza de Vaca ordered one hundred soldiers and two hundred Guaranís to guard the boats while he set off with the rest of the men.

They took with them an Indian guide who had lived there when he was a child. The first day's journey was pleasant. On the fifth day, they came to a river of hot water gushing from a mountain. Then progress became painfully slow. Unusually thick grass barred their way, and a day's chopping through overhanging trees hacked out only a bow-shot length of road.

Knowing the need to move quickly before supplies ran out, Cabeza de Vaca sent an interpreter ahead with the guide to find someone who could take them over the Andes Mountains. They returned with the report that sixteen days away was a person who could lead them to all the gold they could carry.

The goal was in sight, but following proper custom, Cabeza de Vaca consulted with the other officers before making a decision on moving forward. Although he and most of the others were ill with fever, he was unprepared for their refusal to continue. They were concerned because food supplies were perilously low and heavy rains were turning the marshes into endless lakes.

Cabeza de Vaca had endured too much hardship to let such things stop him, but no amount of encouragement on his part persuaded the others to advance. They voted to return to the ships. Believing it would be better to try again the following year, Cabeza de Vaca reluctantly turned back. In doing so, he lost the only opportunity he would ever have to find treasure.

Before abandoning the search, however, he sent two men to gather information about the area where they had intended to go. One went west into the Andes, the other north. Both men returned with tales from the natives that described the Inca empire, but the Spaniards believed it was El Dorado, the mythical city of gold.

The swift current of the Paraguay carried the expedition back to Asunción. Cabeza de Vaca, unaware of the simmering rebellion, arrived on April 8, 1544. Two weeks later shouts of *¡Libertad!* cut short his sleep. The city was in turmoil.

The rebels quickly seized control and arrested Cabeza de Vaca. They hustled him into a small room in the house of one of the leaders of the revolt. Iron shackles were clamped on his legs and five guards set at the door.

Pedro Hernández, Cabeza de Vaca's notary, was ordered to destroy all documents that implicated Irala in wrongdoing. After learning that these papers were in the governor's safe, the crowd broke into Cabeza de Vaca's house and destroyed the papers.

Not content, they took everything there. It was painfully little. They found his velvet court suit, a half-burned candle, a broken sailmaker's needle, a metal syringe, and some items the Indians had given him. They burned his books — one a history of his father's family and the other the story of his adventures on the North American continent.

For more than a year, Cabeza de Vaca was kept chained, his few followers unable to free him. His captors drove posts six feet in the ground so that no one could dig an escape tunnel.

Cabeza de Vaca was not ignorant, however, about the outside world. The woman who brought his food also brought messages. Using a clever magician's trick, she tied tightly-rolled notes under her toes and even brought ink for a response.

It would have pleased his captors if Cabeza de Vaca had simply died — they did not wish to be charged with his murder. But the emaciated governor did not oblige them. He clung to life and to his nerve. When ordered to name Irala as his replacement, he steadfastly insisted that Juan de Salazar would replace him.

Since he would not conveniently die, the rebel leaders found another way to get rid of him. They accused him of crimes against the citizens of Asunción. Using bribery and torture, they had gathered one hundred thirty-two signatures detailing the "wrongs" he had committed. These would accompany the chained executive back to Spain and be laid before the Council of the Indies.

At last the ship was ready to leave. Besides the prisoner, two of the coup leaders were sailing to Spain to present the charges. One was the deposed notary who had with him the long list of complaints.

To make sure that no evidence against them was available for Cabeza de Vaca's defense, Irala's men searched the ship and passengers thoroughly. Satisfied that they were safe, they gave the order for Cabeza de Vaca to be brought aboard.

As the manacled prisoner was carried up the gangplank onto the ship, the officials asked him again to declare Irala as leader in his place. The stubborn conquistador shouted that Salazar was in charge. He was immediately sealed in his cabin.

Suddenly a rock flew in the window. Tied to it was a message from his friends. Unknown to Cabeza de Vaca, they had managed to conceal a list of their grievances against his accusers. He would find it wrapped in waxed cloth hidden in a hollow in one of the beams in the ship's cabin. The document cited the ill treatment the governor had received, and it listed complaints against those who had usurped his authority. There were not nearly as many signatures to this document, but it presented some evidence to the Council of the Indies that there was another side to the story.

At midnight March 7, 1545, less than four years after coming to South America, Cabeza de Vaca left Asunción on his way to Spain to face charges of being a criminal. He had found no gold nor even a route across the Andes. His chains were a testimony to those whose wrath he had incurred by trying to stop abuse of the Indians.

Again the swift current of the Paraguay carried him southward. The ship had gone some distance when another boat drew alongside, and two more prisoners,

Juan de Salazar and Pero Vaca, were taken on board. The rebels in Asunción, in their haste to get rid of them, had given Cabeza de Vaca two more witnesses for his defense.

Once out into the Atlantic, the ship rocked along for two and half months. The lean captive became leaner still when he refused to eat soup in which he discovered two reddish lumps that appeared to him to be poison. He was convinced that his enemies would kill him on the voyage.

Strangely enough, one of his accusers suddenly confessed his part in the whole affair. While the ship was in mid-ocean, he got on his knees and begged Cabeza de Vaca's forgiveness. By the time the trial came, however, the man was so insane that he was unable to act as a witness for either side.

Finally, the ship reached the Azores. Just seven years earlier Cabeza de Vaca had been received with honor on his return from North America, but this time he came ashore in chains. He asked the Portuguese for asylum, and it was granted. He and Salazar sailed to Lisbon on a Portuguese ship.

His captors, who sailed directly to Seville, spread the word that Cabeza de Vaca was a traitor and planned to help Portugal. The destitute governor arrived shortly afterwards, but that did not stop the rumors.

When the Council of the Indies finally met, they considered the long list of signed accusations against the hapless governor. Then they examined the document signed by Cabeza de Vaca's friends. On January 20, 1546, having only this evidence, the judge brought a list of thirty-four charges against Álvar Núñez Cabeza de Vaca.

His crimes seemed so terrible that he was thrown into prison. Shortly, however, this was changed to house arrest at a Madrid inn.

A month later, he stood before the Council for two days. After long testimony, the verdict came swiftly. He was found guilty "on the ground of a sufficient number of witnesses."

His lawyer objected to the decision, and the Cabeza de Vaca was granted three years to prepare a defense. Unfortunately, there were only four witnesses in Spain whom he could call, and one of them was his relative, Pero Vaca. No testimony from anyone living in PARAGUAY was available. It would be another six years before any Spanish ship reached Asunción.

For the next five years, Cabeza de Vaca spent much of the time in court. In some of the suits he was defendant, in others he was the accuser. Then, on March 18, 1551, the verdict was announced in Valladolid. On weight of evidence, he was found guilty, and the judgment was signed and sealed.

The old conquistador, now sixty years old, was not only deprived of the governorship of the Río de la Plata and all the property associated with it, he was forbidden to return to the Indies at all. Instead, he was ordered to serve the king five years in Oran (now ALGERIA), paying the expense for both himself and his horse. He was charged court costs, and, in addition, those who felt he had misused them could sue for damages.

His appeals brought a modification of the sentence. The judgment was changed so that he did not go into military service in Oran, and he was prohibited only from the province of the Río de la Plata. It was probably the king, who knew the conquistador and his service, who lessened the severity of the sentence.

For the rest of his life, Cabeza de Vaca struggled in vain to clear his name. His wife spent her fortune trying to prove the justness of his actions. The last document in the multitude of suits and countersuits filed by or against him is dated November 8, 1555.

That was the year that Pedro Hernández finished writing a history of the Paraguay expedition at the dictation of Cabeza de Vaca. This work was combined with the second edition of his North American adventures and published in Valladolid as *"Relación de los Naufragios y Comentarios.*

The following year the penniless conquistador appealed to the king for aid, and on September 1, 1556, the king sent money to pay for treatment of Cabeza de Vaca's illness. It is likely that he died from this sickness because there is no mention of his name in the records after that.

Cabeza de Vaca had walked on both American continents, but his name is not generally known. He reported no gold from his North American adventures and failed to find it in South America. He failed to find an overland route to Peru. And he had failed in his plan to establish a peaceful coexistence with the Indians.

His humane attitude toward the Indians followed the official policy of the Spanish rulers. But, for the most part, it was men who ignored the policy whose names have gone into the history books.

THE REST OF THE STORY

Of the four survivors of the Narváez Expedition to Florida, the first to die was Estevánico. On returning to Mexico City, he was sold to the Viceroy to scout a route for Coronado's expedition to find the Seven Cities of Gold. Accompanied by a priest named Father Marcos of Nizza, he retraced much of his route. Attended by Indian servants who brought his meals on green dinner plates, he outraced Father Marcos into Hawikuh, reportedly the first of the Seven Cities. At the Zuni pueblo, near the Arizona-New Mexico border, Estevánico sent his source of authority into the mud-walled village. The Zunis reacted angrily at the sight of the gourd rattle decorated with bells and locked him in a house outside the city walls. They killed him when he tried to escape. Father Marcos, in fear of his own life, hurried home with the news. When Coronado reached Hawikuh the following year, he found the green dinner plates and a greyhound Estevánico kept as a pet. Coronado's great search for gold led his men to Grand Canyon, across the Llano Estacado in Texas, and into the plains of Kansas. But there was no gold.

Dorantes had been expected to command the expedition to find the Seven Cities of Gold, but for some reason he did not do it. Instead, he married a wealthy woman, had twelve children, and lived out his life in Mexico.

Castillo, rewarded with half the rent from Tehuacán near Mexico City, lived to a ripe age in luxury.

Those from the Río de la Plata did not fair so well. Irala, two years after sending Cabeza de Vaca back to Spain, took a force of two hundred fifty Spaniards and two thousand Guaranís across the Andes. Peru, however, was already occupied by Spaniards, and the officials in Lima feared this invasion from Paraguay. Irala was forced to leave. Even though the explorers returned to Asunción with no gold, Irala was seen as a strong leader, and his popularity remained high. He died of a pain in his side at the age of forty-five.

Several of Cabeza de Vaca's other enemies either died horrible deaths or were charged with crimes. One was beheaded.

Juan de Salazar, who returned to Asunción, became second in command to Irala, married his daughter, and succeeded him as governor.

Cabeza de Vaca's kinsman, Pero Vaca, returned to South America in 1565 at the age of seventy-five. Penniless, he went to Peru to live with a wealthy brother.

Cabeza de Vaca's wish to provide humane treatment to the Indians in South America found another advocate. In 1609 Jesuit missionaries gathered the Guaranís into communes east of Asunción. Here they lived and worked as equals in a remarkable social experiment. This lasted until 1767, when the Jesuits were expelled from the Spanish colonies.

BIBLIOGRAPHY of SOURCES

Bishop, Morris. *The Odyssey of Cabeza de Vaca*. New York: The Century Company, 1933.

Hallenbeck, Cleve. *Alvar Nunez Cabeza de Vaca: The Journey and Route of the First European to Cross the Continent of North America, 1534-1536*. Clark Company, 1940.

Hedrick, Basil C. and Carroll Riley. *Documents Ancillary to the Vaca Journey*. Carbondale: Southern Illinois University, 1976.

Núñez Cabeza de Vaca, Álvar. *The Account: Alvar Núñez Cabeza de Vaca's Relation*. Ed. by Martin A. Favata and José B. Fernández. Houston: Arte Público Press, 1993.

_____. *Cabeza de Vaca's Adventures in the Unknown Interior of America*. Tr. by Cyclone Covey. Albuquerque: University of New Mexico Press, 1961.

_____. *Castaways: The Narrative of Alvar Nunez Cabeza de Vaca*. Ed. by Enrique Pupo-Walker. Tr. by Frances M. López-Morillas. Berkeley: University of California Press, 1993.

_____. *The Narrative of Alvar Nunez Cabeça de Vaca*. In *Spanish Explorers in the Southern United States, 1528-1543*. Ed. by Frederick W. Hodge. New York: Charles Scribner's Sons, 1907. Texas State Historical Association, 1990.

Rodman, Maia Wojciechowska. *Odyssey of Courage; The Story of Alvar Nunez Cabeza de Vaca*. New York: Atheneum, 1965.

Southey, Robert. *History of Brazil*, Vol. 1. 2d ed. London: Longman, Hurst, Nees, Orme, and Brown. Reprint, Duopage Process.

Terrell, John Upton. *Journey into Darkness*. New York, 1962.

INDEX

*Text set in 12 pt. Times Roman type
with chapter initial letters in 24 pt. Manuscript type
Chapter titles, taken from text of Cabeza de Vaca's books,
set in 36 pt. University Ornate type
Maps by Harold Wade
Cover art by Pat Finney
Printed on 60# Husky recycled paper
Printing and binding by Walsworth Publishing*